75

SPRINGBOARD

POEMS

Springboard

1941-1944

LOUIS MACNEICE

RANDOM HOUSE   NEW YORK

CONTENTS

I

II

NOTE

Many of my titles in this book have the definite article, e.g. "The Satirist," "The Conscript." The reader must not think that I am offering him a set of Theophrastean characters. I am not generalising; "The Conscript" does not stand for all conscripts but for an imagined individual; any such individual seems to me to have an absolute quality which the definite article recognises. Compare the popular use of "the Wife," "the Old Man," "the Baby,"

TO HEDLI

Because the velvet image,
Because the lilting measure,
No more convey my meaning
I am compelled to use
Such words as disabuse
My mind of casual pleasure
And turn it towards a centre—
A zone which others too
And you
May choose to enter.

I

Even poisons praise thee

GEORGE HERBERT

PRAYER BEFORE BIRTH

I am not yet born; O hear me.
Let not the bloodsucking bat or the rat or the stoat or the
    club-footed ghoul come near me.

I am not yet born, console me.
I fear that the human race may with tall walls wall me,
    with strong drugs dope me, with wise lies lure me,
        on black racks rack me, in blood-baths roll me.

I am not yet born; provide me
With water to dandle me, grass to grow for me, trees to talk
    to me, sky to sing to me, birds and a white light
        in the back of my mind to guide me.

I am not yet born; forgive me
For the sins that in me the world shall commit, my words
    when they speak me, my thoughts when they think me,
        my treason engendered by traitors beyond me,
            my life when they murder by means of my
                hands, my death when they live me.

I am not yet born; rehearse me
In the parts I must play and the cues I must take when
    old men lecture me, bureaucrats hector me, mountains
        frown at me, lovers laugh at me, the white
            waves call me to folly and the desert calls
                me to doom and the beggar refuses
                    my gift and my children curse me.

I am not yet born; O hear me,
Let not the man who is beast or who thinks he is God
    come near me.

I am not yet born; O fill me
With strength against those who would freeze my
    humanity, would dragoon me into a lethal automaton,
      would make me a cog in a machine, a thing with
        one face, a thing, and against all those
          who would dissipate my entirety, would
            blow me like thistledown hither and
              thither or hither and thither
                like water held in the
                  hands would spill me.

Let them not make me a stone and let them not spill me.
Otherwise kill me.

PRECURSORS

O that the rain would come—the rain in big battalions—
Or thunder flush the hedge a more clairvoyant green
Or wind walk in and whip us and strip us or booming
Harvest moon transmute this muted scene.

But all is flat, matt, mute, unlivened, unexpectant,
And none but insects dare to sing or pirouette;
That Man is a dancer is an anachronism—
Who has forgotten his steps or hardly learnt them yet.

Yet one or two we have known who had the gusto
Of wind or water-spout, and one or two
Who carry an emerald lamp behind their faces
And—during thunder-storms—the light comes shining through.

EXPLORATIONS

The whale butting through scarps of moving marble,
The tapeworm probing the intestinal darkness,
The swallows drawn collectively to their magnet,
    These are our prototypes and yet,
Though we may envy them still, they are merely patterns
    To wonder at—and forget.

For the ocean-carver, cumbrous but unencumbered,
Who, tired of land, looked for his freedom and frolic in water,
Though he succeeded, has failed; it is only instinct
    That plots his graph and he,
Though appearing to us a free and a happy monster, is merely
    An appanage of the sea.

And the colourless blind worm, triumphantly self-degraded,
Who serves as an image to men of the worst adjustment—
Oxymoron of parasitical glory—
    Cannot even be cursed,
Lacking the only pride of his way of life, not knowing
    That he has chosen the worst.

So even that legion of birds who appear so gladly
Purposeful, with air in their bones, enfranchised
Citizens of the sky and never at odds with
    The season or out of line,
Can be no model to us; their imputed purpose
    Is a foregone design—

And ours is not. For we are unique, a conscious
Hoping and therefore despairing creature, the final
Anomaly of the world, we can learn no method
    From whales or birds or worms;
Our end is our own to be won by our own endeavour
    And held on our own terms.

MUTATIONS

If there has been no spiritual change of kind
Within our species since Cro-Magnon Man
And none is looked for now while the millennia cool,
Yet each of us has known mutations in the mind
When the world jumped and what had been a plan
Dissolved and rivers gushed from what had seemed a pool.

For every static world that you or I impose
Upon the real one must crack at times and new
Patterns from new disorders open like a rose
And old assumptions yield to new sensation;
The Stranger in the wings is waiting for his cue,
The fuse is always laid to some annunciation.

Surprises keep us living: as when the first light
Surprised our infant eyes or as when, very small,
Clutching our parents' hands we toddled down a road
Where all was blank and windless both to touch and sight
Had we not suddenly raised our eyes which showed
The long grass blowing wild on top of the high wall.

For it is true, surprises break and make,
As when the baton falls and all together the hands
On the fiddle-bows are pistons, or when crouched above
His books the scholar suddenly understands
What he has thought for years—or when the inveterate rake
Finds for once that his lust is becoming love.

BROTHER FIRE

When our brother Fire was having his dog's day
Jumping the London streets with millions of tin cans
Clanking at his tail, we heard some shadow say
"Give the dog a bone"—and so we gave him ours;
Night after night we watched him slaver and crunch away
The beams of human life, the tops of topless towers.

Which gluttony of his for us was Lenten fare
Who mother-naked, suckled with sparks, were chill
Though cotted in a grill of sizzling air
Striped like a convict—black, yellow and red;
Thus were we weaned to knowledge of the Will
That wills the natural world but wills us dead.

O delicate walker, babbler, dialectician Fire,
O enemy and image of ourselves,
Did we not on those mornings after the All Clear,
When you were looting shops in elemental joy
And singing as you swarmed up city block and spire,
Echo your thoughts in ours? "Destroy! Destroy!"

THE TROLLS

(Written after an air-raid, April 1941)

(i)

In the misty night humming to themselves like morons
They ramble and rumble over the roof-tops, stumble and
     shamble from pile to pillar,
In clodhopping boots that crunch the stars
And a blank smirk on their faces:
     Pretty Polly won't die yet.

Skittle-alley horseplay, congurgitation . . . they don't know
     what they are doing,
All they can do is stutter and lurch, riding their hobby,
     grinding
Their hobnails into our bodies, into our brains, into the domed
Head where the organ music lingers:
     Pretty Polly won't die yet.

Here they come—I thought we had lost them—
Here they come once more and once too many with their
     rough and
Tumble antics, here they
Are, they are, they ARE:
     Pretty Polly won't die yet,
     Oh, won't she?

(ii)

Than which not any could be found other
And outside which is less than nothing—
This, as they call it, life.
But such as it is, gurgling and tramping, licking their thumbs
     before they

Turn the pages over, tear them out, they
Wish it away, they
Puff with enormous cheeks, put paid to
Hours and minutes—thistledown in the void.

(iii)

Death has a look of finality;
We think we lose something but if it were not for
Death we should have nothing to lose, existence
Because unlimited would merely be existence
Without incarnate value. The trolls can occasion
Our death but they are not able
To use it as we can use it.
Fumbling and mumbling they try to
Spell out Death correctly; they are not able.

(iv)

Than which not any. Time
Swings on the poles of death
And the latitude and the longitude of life
Are fixed by death, and the value
Of every organism, act and moment
Is, thanks to death, unique.

(v)

This then is our answer under
The crawl of lava, a last
Shake of the fist at the vanishing sky, at the hulking
Halfwit demons who rape and slobber, who assume
That when we are killed no more will be heard of us—
Silence of men and trolls' triumph.
A wrong—in the end—assumption.

Barging and lunging out of the clouds, a daft
Descent of no-good gods, they think to
Be rid for ever of the voice of men but they happen
To be trying what even trolls
Can never accomplish, they happen
To be—for all their kudos—
Wrong, wrong in the end.

TROLL'S COURTSHIP

I am a lonely Troll after my gala night;
I have knocked down houses and stamped my feet on the
    people's heart,
I have trundled round the sky with the executioner's cart
And dropped my bait for corpses, watched them bite,
But I am a lonely Troll—nothing in the end comes right.

In a smoking and tinkling dawn with fires and broken glass
I am a lonely Troll; my tributes are in vain
To Her to whom if I had even a human brain
I might have reached but, as it is, the epochs pass
And leave me unfulfilled, no further than I was.

Because I cannot accurately conceive
Any ideal, even ideal Death,
My curses and my boasts are merely a waste of breath,
My lusts and lonelinesses grunt and heave
And blunder round among the ruins that I leave.

Yet from the lubber depths of my unbeing I
Aspire to Her who was my Final Cause but who
Is always somewhere else and not to be spoken to,
Is always nowhere: which is in the long run why
I make for nowhere, make a shambles of the sky.

Nostalgia for the breasts that never gave nor could
Give milk or even warmth has desolated me,
Clutching at shadows of my nullity
That slink and mutter through the leafless wood
Which thanks to me is dead, is dead for good.

A cone of ice enclosing liquid fire,
Utter negation in a positive form,
That would be how She is, the nadir and the norm
Of dissolution and the constant pyre
Of all desirable things—that is what I desire

And therefore cry to Her with the voice of broken bells
To come, visibly, palpably, to come,
Gluing my ear to gutted walls but walls are dumb,
All I can catch is a gurgle as of the sea in shells
But not Her voice—for She is always somewhere else.

CONVOY

Together, keeping in line, slow as if hypnotised
Across the blackboard sea in sombre echelon
The food-ships draw their wakes. No Euclid could have devised
Neater means to a more essential end—
Unless the chalk breaks off, the convoy is surprised.

The cranks go up and down, the smoke-trails tendril out,
The precious cargoes creak, the signals clack,
All is under control and nobody need shout,
We are steady as we go, and on our flanks
The little whippet warships romp and scurry about.

This is a bit like us: the individual sets
A course for all his soul's more basic needs
Of love and pride-of-life, but sometimes he forgets
How much their voyage home depends upon pragmatic
And ruthless attitudes—destroyers and corvettes.

SENTRIES

At the sharp corners of the world, behind
Sandbags or concrete or barbed wire,
Wait the unthinking champions of the mind
Through sombre days or nights of hectic fire;
Without heroics, beautifully uncouth,
Beneath their heavy boots the squelching past
But in their eyes the Future gathering fast
And in their hands unformulated truth.

May these attain to know what they believe,
Live what they know, before the girders part
And chaos drags them under—these naïve
Sentries of the complicated heart.

WHIT MONDAY

Their feet on London, their heads in the grey clouds,
The Bank (if you call it a holiday) Holiday crowds
Stroll from street to street, cocking an eye
For where the angel used to be in the sky;
But the Happy Future is a thing of the past and the street
Echoes to nothing but their dawdling feet.
The Lord's my shepherd—familiar words of myth
Stand up better to bombs than a granite monolith,
Perhaps there is something in them. *I'll not want*—
Not when I'm dead. *He makes me down to lie*—
Death my christening and fire my font—
The quiet (Thames or Don's or Salween's) *waters by*.

1942

SWING-SONG

I'm only a wartime working girl,
The machine shop makes me deaf,
I have no prospects after the war
And *my* young man is in the R.A.F.
    K for Kitty calling P for Prue . . .
    Bomb Doors Open . . .
    Over to You.

Night after night as he passes by
I wonder what he's gone to bomb
And I fancy in the jabber of the mad machines
That I hear him talking on the intercomm.
    K for Kitty calling P for Prue . . .
    Bomb Doors Open . . .
    Over to You.

So there's no one in the world, I sometimes think,
Such a wall flower as I
For I must talk to myself on the ground
While he is talking to his friends in the sky:
    K for Kitty calling P for Prue . . .
    Bomb Doors Open . . .
    Over to You.

BOTTLENECK

Never to fight unless from a pure motive
And for a clear end was his unwritten rule
Who had been in books and visions to a progressive school
And dreamt of barricades, yet being observant
Knew that that was not the way things are:
This man would never make a soldier or a servant.

When I saw him last, carving the longshore mist
With an ascetic profile, he was standing
Watching the troopship leave, he did not speak
But from his eyes there peered a furtive footsore envy
Of these who sailed away to make an opposed landing—
So calm because so young, so lethal because so meek.

Where he is now I could not say; he will,
The odds are, always be non-combatant
Being too violent in soul to kill
Anyone but himself, yet in his mind
A crowd of odd components mutter and press
For compromise with fact, longing to be combined
Into a working whole but cannot jostle through
The permanent bottleneck of his highmindedness.

NEUTRALITY

The neutral island facing the Atlantic,
The neutral island in the heart of man,
Are bitterly soft reminders of the beginnings
That ended before the end began.

Look into your heart, you will find a County Sligo,
A Knocknarea with for navel a cairn of stones,
You will find the shadow and sheen of a moleskin mountain
And a litter of chronicles and bones.

Look into your heart, you will find fermenting rivers,
Intricacies of gloom and glint,
You will find such ducats of dream and great doubloons of
    ceremony
As nobody today would mint.

But then look eastward from your heart, there bulks
A continent, close, dark, as archetypal sin,
While to the west off your own shores the mackerel
Are fat—on the flesh of your kin.

THE CONSCRIPT

Being so young he feels the weight of history
Like clay around his boots; he would, if he could, fly
In search of a future like a sycamore seed
But is prevented by his own Necessity,
His own yet alien, which, whatever he may plead,
To every question gives the same reply.

Choiceless therefore, driven from pillar to post,
Expiating his pedigree, fulfilling
An oracle whose returns grow less and less,
Bandied from camp to camp to practise killing
He fails even so at times to remain engrossed
And is aware, at times, of life's largesse.

From camp to camp, from Eocene to chalk,
He lives a paradox, lives in a groove
That runs dead straight to an ordained disaster
So that in two dimensions he must move
Like an automaton, yet his inward stalk
Vertically aspires and makes him his own master.

Hence, though on the flat his life has no
Promise but of diminishing return,
By feeling down and upwards he can divine
That dignity which far above him burns
In stars that yet are his and which below
Stands rooted like a dolmen in his spine.

NUTS IN MAY

May come up with bird-din
And May come up with sun-dint,
May come up with water-wheels
  And May come up with iris.

In the sun-peppered meadow the shepherds are old,
Their flutes are broken and their tales are told,
And their ears are deaf when the guns unfold
The new philosophy over the wold.

May come up with pollen of death,
May come up with cordite,
May come up with a chinagraph
  And May come up with a stopwatch.

In the high court of heaven Their tail-feathers shine
With cowspit and bullspit and spirits of wine,
They know no pity, being divine,
And They give no quarter to thine or mine.

May come up with Very lights,
May come up with duty,
May come up with a bouncing cheque,
  An acid-drop and a bandage.

Yes, angels are frigid and shepherds are dumb,
There is no holy water when the enemy come,
The trees are askew and the skies are a-hum
And you have to keep mum and go to it and die for your life and
  keep mum.

May come up with fiddle-bows,
May come up with blossom,
May come up the same again,
  The same again but different.

THE MIXER

With a pert moustache and a ready candid smile
He has played his way through twenty years of pubs,
Deckchairs, lounges, touchlines, junctions, homes,
And still as ever popular, he roams
Far and narrow, mimicking the style
Of other people's leisure, scattering stubs.

Colourless, when alone, and self-accused,
He is only happy in reflected light
And only real in the range of laughter;
Behind his eyes are shadows of a night
In Flanders but his mind long since refused
To let that time intrude on what came after.

So in this second war which is fearful too,
He cannot away with silence but has grown
Almost a cypher, like a Latin word
That many languages have made their own
Till it is worn and blunt and easy to construe
And often spoken but no longer heard.

NOSTALGIA

In cock-wattle sunset or grey
Dawn when the dagger
Points again of longing
For what was never home
We needs must turn away
From the voices that cry "Come"—
That under-sea ding-donging.

Dingle-dongle, bells and bluebells,
Snapdragon solstice, lunar lull,
The wasp circling the honey
Or the lamp soft on the snow—
These are the times at which
The will is vulnerable,
The trigger-finger slow,
The spirit lonely.

These are the times at which
Aloneness is too ripe
When homesick for the hollow
Heart of the Milky Way
The soundless clapper calls
And we would follow
But earth and will are stronger
And nearer—and we stay.

BABEL

There was a tower that went before a fall.
    Can't we ever, my love, speak in the same language?
Its nerves grew worse and worse as it grew tall.
    Have we no aims in common?

As children we were bickering over beads—
    Can't we ever, my love, speak in the same language?
The more there are together, Togetherness recedes.
    Have we no aims in common?

Exiles all as we are in a foreign city,
    Can't we ever, my love, speak in the same language?
We cut each other's throats out of our great self-pity—
    Have we no aims in common?

Patriots, dreamers, die-hards, theoreticians, all,
    Can't we ever, my love, speak in the same language,
Or shall we go, still quarrelling over words, to the wall?
    Have we no aims in common?

SCHIZOPHRENE

Hearing offstage the taps filling the bath
The set dissolves to childhood—in her cot
Hearing that ominous relentless noise
Which the grown-ups have started, who are not
She knows, aware of what it means; it means
The Dark, the Flood, the Malice. It destroys
All other meanings—dolls or gingerbread;
It means a Will that wills all children dead.

Hearing the gasfire breathe monotonously
She waits for words but no words come, she lifts
A soapstone hand to smooth her hair and feels
The hand is someone else's—the scene shifts
To a cold desert where the wind has dropped
And the earth's movement stopped and something steals
Up from the grit through nerve and bone and vein
To flaunt its iron tendrils in her brain.

Hearing again the telegraph wires again
Humming again and always, she must lean
Against the humming post and search her mind
For what it is they say; in some latrine
She knows she wrote it first upon the wall
In self-incrimination, duly signed;
And, unrevoked since then, that signature
Runs round the world on wires, accusing her.

Hearing the church-bells too, she knows at once
That only she can hear them for it is no
Church or even belfry where they hang,
There are no ropes attached or ringers down below,

These bells are disembodied, they express
The claims of frozen Chaos and will clang
Till this and every other world shall melt
And Chaos be Itself and nothing felt.

Lastly, hearing the cock in the grey dawn
Crow once, crow twice, she shivers and dissolves
To someone else who in the hour of trial
Denied his Master and his guilt devolves
On her head only. If she could speak up,
She might even now atone for that denial
But the grey cock still crows and she knows why;
For she must still deny, deny, deny.

ALCOHOL

On golden seas of drink, so the Greek poet said,
Rich and poor are alike. Looking around in war
We watch the many who have returned to the dead
Ordering time-and-again the same-as-before:

Those Haves who cannot bear making a choice,
Those Have-nots who are bored with having nothing to choose,
Call for their drinks in the same tone of voice,
Find a factitious popular front in booze.

Another drink: Bacchylides was right
And self-deception golden—Serve him quick,
The siphon stutters in the archaic night,
The flesh is willing and the soul is sick.

Another drink: Adam is back in the Garden.
Another drink: the snake is back on the tree.
Let your brain go soft, your arteries will harden;
If God's a peeping tom he'll see what he shall see.

Another drink: Cain has slain his brother.
Another drink: Cain, they say, is cursed.
Another and another and another—
The beautiful ideologies have burst.

A bottle swings on a string. The matt-grey iron ship,
Which ought to have been the Future, sidles by
And with due auspices descends the slip
Into an ocean where no auspices apply.

Take away your slogans; give us something to swallow,
Give us beer or brandy or schnapps or gin;
This is the only road for the self-betrayed to follow—
The last way out that leads not out but in.

THE LIBERTINE

In the old days with married women's stockings
Twisted round his bedpost he felt himself a gay
Dog but now his liver has begun to groan,
Now that pick-ups are the order of the day:
O leave me easy, leave me alone.

Voluptuary in his 'teens and cynic in his twenties,
He ran through women like a child through growing hay
Looking for a lost toy whose capture might atone
For his own guilt and the cosmic disarray:
O leave me easy, leave me alone.

He never found the toy and has forgotten the faces,
Only remembers the props . . . a scent-spray
Beside the bed or a milk-white telephone
Or through the triple ninon the acrid trickle of day:
O leave me easy, leave me alone.

Long fingers over the gunwale, hair in a hair-net,
Furs in January, cartwheel hats in May,
And after the event the wish to be alone—
Angels, goddesses, bitches, all have edged away:
O leave me easy, leave me alone.

So now, in middle age, his erotic programme
Torn in two, if after such a delay
An accident should offer him his own
Fulfilment in a woman, still he would say:
O leave me easy, leave me alone.

EPITAPH FOR LIBERAL POETS

If in the latter
End—which is fairly soon—our way of life goes west
And some shall say So What and some What Matter,
Ready under new names to exploit or be exploited,
What, though better unsaid, would we have history say
Of us who walked in our sleep and died on our Quest?

We who always had, but never admitted, a master,
Who were expected—and paid—to be ourselves,
Conditioned to think freely, how can we
Patch up our broken hearts and modes of thought in plaster
And glorify in chromium-plated stories
Those who shall supersede us and cannot need us—
The tight-lipped technocratic Conquistadores?

The Individual has died before; Catullus
Went down young, gave place to those who were born old
And more adaptable and were not even jealous
Of his wild life and lyrics. Though our songs
Were not so warm as his, our fate is no less cold.

Such silence then before us, pinned against the wall,
Why need we whine? There is no way out, the birds
Will tell us nothing more; we shall vanish first,
Yet leave behind us certain frozen words
Which some day, though not certainly, may melt
And, for a moment or two, accentuate a thirst.

THE SATIRIST

Who is that man with the handshake? Don't you know?
He is the pinprick master, he can dissect
All your moods and manners, he can discover
A selfish motive for anything—and collect
His royalties as recording angel. No
Reverence here for hero, saint or lover.

Who is that man so deftly filling his pipe
As if creating something? That's the reason:
He is not creative at all, his mind is dry
And bears no blossoms even in the season,
He is an onlooker, a heartless type,
Whose hobby is giving everyone else the lie.

Who is that man with eyes like a lonely dog?
Lonely is right. He knows that he has missed
What others miss unconsciously. Assigned
To a condemned ship he still must keep the log
And so fulfil the premises of his mind
Where large ideals have bred a satirist.

THIS WAY OUT

You're not going yet? I must; I have to work.
Though no one better relished halcyon days
Behind his eyes the winch of will was busy
And dizzy ways led zigzag through the murk.

So deprecatingly he blew a nought
In smoke and threw the stub into the purring grate
And left us, as he always did, to follow
His colonising fate through Africas of thought.

He always broke off so, abrupt but shy
In knowledge of his mission, veered and tacked
To his own breezes—till as a variation
His explanation cracked and threw the words awry:
You're not going yet? I must; I have to die.

THYESTES

When the King sat down to the feast and the golden lid
    revealed
The human cutlets and the Graces sang
Their lays of love returned and lovers meeting,
Did his blood tell him what his mind concealed?
Didn't he know—or did he—what he was eating?

Thus Here and We, neither of which is what
The mind and map admit, in perfidy are linked;
This green foam frets away our sense of duty
While we, who watch it blossom and bulge, are not
Spectators in our hearts but murderers of beauty.

Cannibalism and incest: such is time,
A trail of shaking candles, such are we
Who garnish to pollute and breed to kill—
Messmates in the eucharist of crime
And heirs to two of those three black crosses on the hill.

PRAYER IN MID-PASSAGE

O Thou my monster, Thou my guide,
Be with me where the bluffs divide
Nor let me contemplate return
To where my backward chattels burn
In haunts of friendship and untruth—
The Cities of the Plain of Youth.

O pattern of inhuman good,
Hard critic of our thought and blood,
By whose decree there is no zone
Where man can live by men alone,
Unveil Thyself that all may see
Thy fierce impersonality.

We were the past—and doomed because
We were a past that never was;
Yet grant to men that they may climb
This time-bound ladder out of time
And by our human organs we
Shall thus transcend humanity.

Take therefore, though Thou disregard,
This prayer, this hymn, this feckless word,
O Thou my silence, Thou my song,
To whom all focal doubts belong
And but for whom this breath were breath—
Thou my meaning, Thou my death.

PROSPECT

Though loves languish and sour
Fruit puts the teeth on edge,
Though the ragged nests are empty of song
In the barbed and blistered hedge,

Though old men's lives and children's bricks
Spell out a Machiavellian creed,
Though the evil Past is ever present
And the happy Present is past indeed,

Though the stone grows and grows
That we roll up the hill
And the hill grows and grows
And gravity conquers still,

Though Nature's laws exploit
And defeat anarchic men,
Though every sandcastle concept
Being *ad hoc* must crumble again,

And though today is arid,
We know—and knowing bless—
That rooted in futurity
There is a plant of tenderness.

THE SPRINGBOARD

He never made the dive—not while I watched.
High above London, naked in the night
Perched on a board. I peered up through the bars
Made by his fear and mine but it was more than fright
That kept him crucified among the budding stars.

Yes, it was unbelief. He knew only too well
That circumstances called for sacrifice
But, shivering there, spreadeagled above the town,
His blood began to haggle over the price
History would pay if he were to throw himself down.

If it would mend the world, that would be worth while
But he, quite rightly, long had ceased to believe
In any Utopia or in Peace-upon-Earth;
His friends would find in his death neither ransom nor reprieve
But only a grain of faith—for what it was worth.

And yet we know he knows what he must do.
There above London where the gargoyles grin
He will dive like a bomber past the broken steeple,
One man wiping out his own original sin
And, like ten million others, dying for the people.

II

Lascio lo fele e vo per dolci pomi

DANTE

II

THE CASUALTY
(*in memoriam G.H.S.*)

"Damn!" you would say if I were to write the best
Tribute I could to you, "All clichés," and you would grin
Dwindling to where that faded star allures
Where no time presses and no days begin—
Turning back shrugging to the misty West
Remembered out of Homer but now yours.

Than whom I do not expect ever again
To find a more accordant friend, with whom
I could be silent knowledgeably; you never
Faked or flattered or time-served. If ten
Winds were to shout you down or twenty oceans boom
Above the last of you, they will not sever

That thread of so articulate silence. How
You died remains conjecture; instantaneous
Is the most likely—that the shutter fell
Congealing the kaleidoscope at Now
And making all your past contemporaneous
Under that final chord of the mid-Atlantic swell.

So now the concert is over, the seats vacated,
Eels among the footlights, water up to the roof
And the gilded cherubs crumbling—and you come in
Jaunty as ever but with a half-frustrated
Look on your face, you expect the show to begin
But you are too late and cannot accept the proof

That you are too late because you have died too early
And this is under sea. Puzzled but gay
You still come in, come in, and the waves distort
Your smile and chivvy your limbs through a maze of pearly
Pillars of ocean death—and yet you force your way
In on my dreams as if you had something still to report.

[49]

How was it then? How is it? You and I
Have often since we were children discussed death
And sniggered at the preacher and wondered how
He can talk so big about mortality
And immortality more. But you yourself could now
Talk big as any—if you had the breath.

However since you cannot from this date
Talk big or little, since you cannot answer
Even what alive you could, but I let slip
The chance to ask you, I can correlate
Only of you what memories dart and trip
Through freckling lights and stop like a forgetful dancer.

Archaic gusto sprouted from a vase
Of dancing satyrs, lips of a Gothic imp
Laughing down from a church-top, inky fingers
Jotting notes on notes, and piccolo and tymp
Importunate at the circus—but there lingers
Also a scent of awe, a cosmic pause;

For you were a good mixer and could laugh
With Rowlandson or Goya and you liked
Bijoux and long-eared dogs and silken legs
And titivated rooms but more than half
Your story lay outside beyond the spiked
Railing where in the night the blinded minstrel begs.

He begged and you responded, being yourself,
Like Raftery or Homer, of his kind—
Creative not for the counter or the shelf
But innocently whom the world bewilders
And so they observe and love it till their mind
May turn them from mere students into builders.

[50]

Of which high humble company were you,
Outside the cliques, unbothered with the fashion,
And self-apprenticed to the grinding trade
Of thinking things anew, stropping the blade
You never used, your multicoloured passion
Having been merged by death in universal Blue.

So what you gave were inklings: trivial signs
Of some momentous truth, a footprint here and there
In melting snow, a marginal caress
Of someone else's words, a gentleness
In greeting, a panache of heady wines
Or children's rockets vanishing in air.

Look at these snapshots; here you see yourself
Spilling a paint-pot on a virgin wall
Or boisterous in a sailing-boat or bubbling
At a Punch-and-Judy show or a music-hall
Or lugging Clausewitz from a public shelf
To make your private notes, thumbing and doubling

His corseted pages back. Yes, here and here
You see yourself spilling across the border
Of nice convention, here at a students' dance
Pinching a girl's behind—to reappear
A small boy twined in bracken and aprance
Like any goatfoot faun to propagate disorder.

Here you are swapping gags in winking bars
With half an eye on the colour clash of beet
Lobster and radish, here you are talking back
To a caged baboon and here the Wilshire sleet
Riddles your football jersey—here the sack
Of night pours down on you Provençal stars.

Here you are gabbling Baudelaire or Donne,
Here you are mimicking that cuckoo clock,
Here you are serving a double fault for set,
Here you are diving naked from a Dalmatian rock,
Here you are barracking the sinking sun,
Here you are taking Proust aboard your doomed corvette.

Yes, all you gave were inklings; even so
Invaluable—such as I remember
Out of your mouth or only in your eyes
On walks in blowsy August, Brueghel-like December,
Or when the gas was hissing and a glow
Of copper jugs gave back your lyrical surprise.

For above all that was your gift—to be
Surprised and therefore sympathetic, warm
Towards things as well as people, you could see
The integrity of differences—O did you
Make one last integration, find a Form
Grow out of formlessness when the Atlantic hid you?

Whether you did or not, the fact remains
(Though you yourself might think it nothing to shout of)
That all your life till then showed an endeavour
Towards a discovery—and if your pains
Were lost the loss is ours as well; for you are out of
This life and cannot start any more hares for ever.

THE NEWS-REEL

Since Munich, what? A tangle of black film
Squirming like bait upon the floor of my mind
And scissors clicking daily. I am inclined
To pick these pictures now but will hold back
Till memory has elicited from this blind
Drama its threads of vision, the intrusions
Of value upon fact, that sudden unconfined
Wind of understanding that blew out
From people's hands and faces, undesigned
Evidence of design, that change of climate
Which did not last but happens often enough
To give us hope that fact is a façade
And that there is an organism behind
Its brittle littleness, a rhythm and a meaning,
Something half-conjectured and half-divined,
Something to give way to and so find.

THE KINGDOM

(i)

Under the surface of flux and of fear there is an underground
   movement,
Under the crust of bureaucracy, quiet behind the posters,
Unconscious but palpably there—the Kingdom of individuals.

And of these is the Kingdom—
Equal in difference, interchangeably sovereign—
The incorruptible souls who work without a commission,
The pairs of hands that are peers of hearts, the eyes that marry
   with eyes,
The candid scholar, the unselfish priest, the uncomplaining
   mothers of many,
The active men who are kind, the contemplative who give,
The happy-go-lucky saint and the peace-loving buccaneer.

These, as being themselves, are apart from not each other
But from such as being false are merely other,
So these are apart as parts within a pattern
Not merged nor yet excluded, members of a Kingdom
Which has no king except each subject, therefore
Apart from slaves and tyrants and from every
Community of mere convenience; these are
Apart from those who drift and those who force,
Apart from partisan order and egotistical anarchy,
Apart from the easy religion of him who would find in God
A boss, a ponce, an alibi, and apart from
The logic of him who arrogates to himself
The secret of the universe, the whole
Choreography of atoms; these are humble
And proud at once, working within their limits
And yet transcending them. These are the people

Who vindicate the species. And they are many. For go,
Go wherever you choose, among tidy villas or terrible
Docks, dumps and pitheads, or through the spangled moors
Or along the vibrant narrow intestines of great ships
Or into those countries of which we know very little—
Everywhere you will discover the men of the Kingdom
Loyal by intuition, born to attack, and innocent.

(ii)

Take this old man with the soldierly straight back
Dressed in tweeds like a squire but he has not a squire's
    presumption,
His hands are gentle with wild flowers, his memory
Latticed with dialect and anecdotes
And wisps of nature poetry; he is of the Kingdom,
A country-lover and very English, the cadence
Of Christmas bells in his voice, his face like Cotswold stone
Severe but warm, a sureness in his walk
And his blood attuned to the seasons—whether it is the glyptic
Winter turning feathered twigs to stone
And making the Old Bill pollards monuments
Beside the dyke of Lethe—or if it is the frantic
Calf-love and early oratory of spring—
Or peony-time with the midges dancing—or later, sweeter,
That two-in-one of clarity and mist,
Of maidenlight and ripeness which is autumn:
Every case is new and yet he knows the answers
For he is of the Kingdom. Through the serene and chequered
Fields that he knows he walks like a fallen angel
Whose fall has made him a man. Ladders of cirrhus cloud
Lead down as well as up, the ricochet of rain
Makes the clay smell sweet and snow in sunlight
Affirms the tussocks under it. Such changes—
The hedgerow stippled with hips or lathered with elder—

To him are his own rhythm like his breathing
And intimate as dreams. Hirsute or fluted earth,
Squares of plough and stubble, oatcake and corduroy,
Russet and emerald, and the shot-silk evening
And all the folk-song stars—these are his palette
And it is he who blends them with the brush-strokes
Of long experience and sudden insight,
Being mature and yet naïve, a lover
Of what is not himself—but it becomes himself
And he repays it interest, so has had
A happy life and will die happy; more—
Belongs, though he never knew it, to the Kingdom.

(iii)

When she had her stroke the china dogs
Did not even flinch, although they might have guessed
That tomorrow no one would dust them, but the family
Felt that this was an Act of God and did not see
The syllogism slouched across the kitchen table,
The inevitable caller; given poverty,
Given two on the dole and one a cripple,
Given the false peace and the plight of England,
And given her matriarchal pride, her bones
That would not rest, her arrogation of every
Job in the house to herself, given her grim
Good humour—her daily tonic against despair,
Given her wakeful nights trying to balance the budget
And given her ignorance of her own frailty,
What other end was coming? They propped her up
While the canary fidgeted with his seed
And the clock hiccuped, being about to strike,
And someone ran for the doctor: "Our Mother is taken bad."
Everything in that house was mutually possessive:
She was Our Mother, Dad was called Our Dad,

Connie Our Connie and the cat Our Tiger
But now the most possessing and the most possessed
Was on her way to leave them. They did not see
Even that this was so, they did not see
The tall clock stretch his arms like a rising Cross
Or see the steam of the kettle turn to incense;
Our Mother is taken bad—and that was all.
They did not see that the only cable was broken
That held them together, self-respecting and sane,
And that chaos was now on the move. For they did not know,
Except at times by inklings, that their home
Remained a rebel island in the sea
Of authorised disgust only because their mother
Who thought herself resigned, was a born rebel
Against the times and loyal to a different
Order, being enfranchised of the Kingdom.

(iv)

"Drunk again! Where do you think you are?"
"I think I am somewhere where I don't belong;
I chanced in here from the Kingdom." And he crashed
His heavyweight hand among the chipped and dinted
Vessels of false good-fellowship, went out
Into the night with his chin like a bulldozer
Churning a trough of fury; then the Night
Being herself archaic and instinctive
Welcomed his earthy anger, slapped him on the back
And told him stories that were not wit but humour,
Not smut but satyr-talk, not clever but wise,
Not elegant but poetry. And his mouth relaxed,
His head went back and he laughed, hearing the bugle
That blows tomorrow morning, blows for a hard routine,
Blows for the life automatic, for spit and polish and jargon
And deference to fools, but blows also for comrades.

Blows for a gay and a brave unforced solidarity,
Blows for the elemental community, blows for
Knowledge of shared emotion past and future,
(Blows for the static life that suddenly comes to
Life with the smell at dawn of running engines)
And blows as well—to those who have ears to hear
And hands to strike—for the Kingdom.

(v)

Too large in feature for a world of cuties,
Too sculptured for a cocktail lounge flirtation,
This girl is almost awkward, carrying off
The lintel of convention on her shoulders,
A Doric river-goddess with a pitcher
Of ice-cold wild emotions. Pour them where she will
The pitcher will not empty nor the stream grow warm
But is so cold it burns. Vitality and fear
Are marbled in her eyes, from hour to hour
She changes like the sky—one moment is so gay
That all her words are laughter but the next
Moment she is puzzled, her own Sphinx,
Made granite by her destiny, encumbered
With the dour horoscopes of dying nations
Deduced from dying stars.
So what can you expect? Behind that classic
Forehead, under that smooth Renaissance dome,
The Gothic devils revel around a corpse
Allegedly a saint's and snuff the holy candles
And cackle and deny—and their denial
Torments her with a doubt. She raises once again
Her pitcher, tilts it—Will the water flow?—
And see, it flows, it flows, ice-cold as ever,
Anarchic, pure and healing. For she filled it
One day that is not dead at a lost well

Between two rocks under a sombre ilex
In the grey dawn in a deserted corner
Of the remembered Kingdom.

(vi)

A little dapper man but with shiny elbows
And short keen sight, he lived by measuring things
And died like a recurring decimal
Run off the page, refusing to be curtailed;
Died as they say in harness, still believing
In science, reason, progress. Left his work
Unfinished *ipso facto* which continued
Will supersede his name in the next text-book
And relegate him to the anonymous crowd
Of small discoverers in lab or cloister
Who link us with the Ice Age. Obstinately
He canalised his fervour, it was slow
The task he set himself but plotting points
On graph paper he felt the emerging curve
Like the first flutterings of an embryo
In somebody's first pregnancy; resembled
A pregnant woman too in that his logic
Yet made that hidden child the centre of the world
And almost a messiah; so that here
Even here over the shining test-tubes
The spirit of the alchemist still hovered
Hungry for magic, for the philosopher's stone.
And Progress—is that magic too? He never
Would have conceded it, not even in these last
Years of endemic doubt; in his perspective
Our present tyrants shrank into parochial
Lords of Misrule, cross eddies in a river
That has to reach the sea. But has it? Who
Told him the sea was there?

Maybe he told himself and the mere name
Of Progress was a shell to hold to the ear
And hear the breakers burgeon. Rules were rules
And all induction checked but in the end
His reasoning hinged on faith and the first axiom
Was oracle or instinct. He was simple
This man who flogged his brain, he was a child;
And so, whatever progress means in general,
He in his work meant progress. Patiently
As Stone Age man he flaked himself away
By blocked-out patterns on a core of flint
So that the core which was himself diminished
Until his friends complained that he had lost
Something in charm or interest. But conversely
His mind developed like an ancient church
By the accretion of side-aisles and the enlarging of lights
Till all the walls are windows and the sky
Comes in, if coloured; such a mind . . . a man . . .
Deserves a consecration; such a church
Bears in its lines the trademark of the Kingdom.

(vii)

All is well, said the voice from the tiny pulpit,
All is well with the child. And the voice cracked
For the preacher was very old and the coffin down in the aisle
Held the body of one who had been his friend and colleague
For forty years and was dead in daffodil time
Before it had come to Easter. All is well with
One who believed and practised and whose life
Presumed the Resurrection. What that means
He may have felt he knew; this much is certain—
The meaning filled his actions, made him courteous
And lyrical and strong and kind and truthful,
A generous puritan. Above whose dust

About this time each year the spendthrift plants
Will toss their trumpets heralding a life
That shows itself in time but remains timeless
As is the heart of music. So today
These yellow fanfares in the trench re-echo,
Before the spades get busy, the same phrase
The preacher lost his voice on. All is well,
The flowers say, with the child; and so it must be
For, it is said, the children are of the Kingdom.

(viii)

Over the roofs and cranes, blistered cupola and hungry smoke-
    stack, over the moored balloons and the feathery tufts of
    searchlights,
Over the cold transmitters jabbering under the moon,
Over the hump of the ocean big with wrecks and over
Our hide-bound fog-bound lives the hosts of the living collect
Like migrant birds, or bees to the sound of a gong:
Subjects all of the Kingdom but each in himself a king.
These are the people who know in their bones the answer
To the statesman's quiz and the false reformer's crude
Alternatives and ultimatums. These have eyes
And can see each other's goodness, do not need salvation
By whip, brochure, sterilisation or drugs,
Being incurably human; these are the catalytics
To break the inhuman into humanity; these are
The voices whose words, whether in code or in clear,
Are to the point and can be received apart from
The buzz of jargon. Apart from the cranks, the timid,
The self-deceiving realist, the self-seeking
Altruist, the self-indulgent penitent,
Apart from all the frauds are these who have the courage
Of their own vision and their friends' good will
And have not lost their cosmic pride, responding

[61]

Both to the simple lyrics of blood and the architectonic fugues
  of reason.
These have their faults like all creators, like
The hero who must die or like the artist who
Himself is like a person with one hand
Working it into a glove; yes, they have faults
But are the chosen—because they have chosen, being
Beautiful if grotesque and wise though wilful
And hard as meteorites. Of these, of such is
Your hope, your clue, your cue, your snowball letter
That makes your soft flakes hard, your aspirations active;
Of such is your future if it is to be fruitful,
Of such is your widow's cruse, your Jacob's ladder,
Of such is the garden of souls, the orchestration of instinct,
The fertilisation of mind, of such are your beacons,
Your breaking of bread, your dance of desire, your North-
  West passage,
Of such is the epilogue to your sagas of bronze and steel,
Your amnesty, your advent, your Rebirth,
The archetype and the vindication of history;
The hierarchy of the equal—the Kingdom of Earth.

POSTSCRIPT

When we were children words were coloured
(Harlot and murder were dark purple)
And language was a prism, the light
    A conjured inlay on the grass,
Whose rays today are concentrated
    And language grown a burning-glass.

When we were children Spring was easy,
Dousing our heads in suds of hawthorn
And scrambling the laburnum tree—
    A breakfast for the gluttonous eye;
Whose winds and sweets have now forsaken
    Lungs that are black, tongues that are dry.

Now we are older and our talents
Accredited to time and meaning,
To handsel joy requires a new
    Shuffle of cards behind the brain
Where meaning shall remarry colour
    And flowers be timeless once again.

June, 1944

75
76
77
79
83
85